Bradford

Bradford

Clive Hardy

Waterton Press Limited

First published in the United Kingdom in 1999 by
Frith Publishing an imprint of Waterton Press Limited

British Library Cataloguing in Publication Data

Clive Hardy
Bradford

ISBN 1-84125-087-2

Reproductions of all the photographs in this book are
available as framed or mounted prints. For more
information please contact The Francis Frith Collection
at the address below quoting the title of this book and
the page number and photograph number or title.

The Francis Frith Collection,
'Friths Barn', Teffont, Salisbury, Wiltshire, SP3 5QP
Tel: 01722 716376
E mail: bookprints@francisfrith.com
Web pages: www.francisfrith.com

Typeset in Bembo Semi Bold

Printed and bound in Great Britain by
WBC Limited, Bridgend, Glamorgan.

Contents

Francis Frith 1822–1898

Introduction
Francis Frith: A Victorian Pioneer

Francis Frith, the founder of the world famous photographic archive was a complex and multitudinous man. A devout Quaker and a highly successful and respected Victorian businessman he was also a flamboyant character.

By 1855 Frith had already established a wholesale grocery business in Liverpool and sold it for the astonishing sum of £200,000, equivalent of over £15,000,000 today. Now a multi-millionaire he was able to indulge in his irresistible desire to travel. As a child he had pored over books penned by early explorers, and his imagination had been stirred by family holidays to the sublime mountain regions of Wales and Scotland. "What a land of spirit-stirring and enriching scenes and places!" he had written. He was to return to these scenes of grandeur in later years to "recapture the thousands of vivid and tender memories", but with a very different purpose. Now in his thirties, and captivated by the new science of photography, Frith set out on a series of pioneering journeys to the Middle East, that occupied him from 1856 until 1860.

He took with him a specially-designed wicker carriage which acted as camera, dark-room and sleeping chamber. These far-flung journeys were full of intrigue and adventure. In his life story, written when he was sixty-three, Frith tells of being held captive by bandits, and fighting "an awful midnight battle to the very point of exhaustion and surrender with a deadly pack of hungry, wild dogs". He bargained for several weeks with a "mysterious priest" over a beautiful seven-volume illuminated Koran, which is now in the British Museum. Wearing full arab costume, Frith arrived at Akaba by camel seventy years before Lawrence of Arabia, where he encountered "desert princes and rival sheikhs, blazing with jewel-hilted swords".

During these extraordinary adventures he was assiduously exploring the desert regions of the Nile and recording the antiquities and people with his camera, Frith was the first photographer ever to travel beyond the sixth cataract. Africa, we must remember, was still the "Dark Continent", and Stanley and Livingstone's famous meeting was a decade into the future. The conditions for picture taking confound belief. He laboured for hours on end in his dark-room in the sweltering heat, while the volatile collodion chemicals fizzed dangerously in their trays. Often he was forced to work in tombs and caves where conditions were cooler.

Back in London he exhibited his photographs and was "rapturously cheered" by the Royal Society. His reputation as a photographer was made overnight. His photographs were issued in albums by James S. Virtue and William MacKenzie, and published simultaneously in London and New York. An eminent historian has likened their impact on the population of the time to that on our own generation of the first photographs taken on the surface of the moon.

Characteristically, Frith spotted the potential to create a new business as a specialist publisher of photographs. In 1860 he married Mary Ann Rosling and set out to photograph every city, town and village in Britain. For the next thirty years Frith travelled the country by train and by pony and trap, producing photographs that were keenly bought by the millions of Victorians who, because of the burgeoning rail network, were beginning to enjoy holidays and day trips to Britain's seaside resorts and beauty spots.

To meet the demand he gathered together a team of up to twelve photographers, and also published the work of independent artist-photographers of the reputation of Roger Fenton and Francis Bedford. Together with clerks and photographic printers he employed a substantial staff at his Reigate studios. To gain an understanding of the scale of Frith's business one only has to look at the catalogue issued by Frith & Co. in 1886. It runs to some 670 pages listing not only many thousands of views of the British Isles but also photographs of most major European countries, and China, Japan, the USA and Canada. By 1890 Frith had created the greatest specialist photographic publishing company in the world.

He died in 1898 at his villa in Cannes, his great project still growing. His sons, Eustace and Cyril, took over the task, and Frith & Co. continued in business for another seventy years, until by 1970 the archive contained over a third of a million pictures of 7,000 cities, towns and villages.

The photographic record he has left to us stands as a living monument to a remarkable and very special man.

Frith's dhow in Egypt *c.*1857

CHAPTER 1

∽ BRADFORD ∽

Many of the photographs appearing in this selection from the Frith Collection were taken in the 1880s and 90s. It was a time when Bradford was the centre of the woollen and worsted industry, not only in this country but throughout the world. However, the city's manufacturers were suffering from the effects of import tariffs imposed by a number of European countries – and there was worse to come. The Mckinley Tariffs of 1895 resulted in the halving of British woollen and worsted exports to the USA. Even so, the late-Victorian traveller would have found the city a veritable forest of smoking mill chimneys interspersed with the often squalid housing of the workers. Streams and brooks ran black, polluted with mill waste and sewage.

There were other industries too. Bradford was on the western edge of the great Yorkshire coalfield and because the coal was near to the surface, it could be mined relatively inexpensively. Also close by were the ironworks of Bowling and Low Moor. For centuries Bradford had grown slowly. The first written account we have comes from the *Domesday Book*. The entry covers the village itself together with several outlying hamlets and a number of manors. The total population was almost certainly less than one thousand, of which a couple of hundred or so would be living in Bradford. The biggest landowner in the area was a man named Gamel. Of Norse descent, Gamel farmed a number of plots throughout the area, which amounted to 1,500 acres.

∽ BRADFORD AND THE WOOLLEN INDUSTRY ∽

Just when Bradford's association with the woollen industry began is unknown. However, we do know that some weaving was being carried out in the area during the late-thirteenth century, as an Inquisition from that era mentions the fining and imprisonment of one Evan of Gumersal, a weaver. In other parts of the county, cloth-making was fairly widespread, though on a small scale. The only exceptions to this were York and later Beverley, both of which had weaving guilds, the former as early as 1150.

Without doubt the major influence on Yorkshire's medieval development was the great Cistercian abbeys, such as Fountains, Rievaulx, Jervaulx and Kirkstall. Founded in poverty, the abbeys grew rich and powerful thanks to generous donations of land from Norman lords. It was on these lands that the abbeys reared sheep for their wool; at one time Fountains Abbey had 600,000 acres devoted to sheep pasture.

Most English wool was not woven at home but exported to Flanders and Lombardy. In order to finance some of their building programmes, monasteries would sell several years' wool production in advance by means of forward contracts. Sometimes this went wrong, leaving the monks well and truly in the red. In 1275 the Jews of York bailed out Fountains Abbey, which was over £6,000 in debt – a phenomenal amount of money in those days.

The abbey most closely associated with Bradford was Kirkstall. Founded under the patronage of Henry de Lacy, Lord of Pontefract, the monks of Kirkstall had first settled at Barnoldswick-in-Craven, but moved to the banks of the Aire in 1152. Kirkstall was given lands around Bradford and the charter to hold Wibsey Fair.

The fourteenth century saw a significant increase in the amount of cloth woven in England and the export of manufactured cloth to the Continent. This was due to a number of factors, including the introduction of the spinning wheel into more rural areas, and a policy that actively encouraged Flemish weavers to come and settle in Yorkshire. For the most part the type of cloth produced was only one yard wide; anything wider required a broadloom, which had to be worked by two men.

Towards the latter part of the seventeenth century the spinning of worsted yarn gained a foothold around Halifax and Bradford. Apparently there had been some production in Yorkshire as early as the fourteenth century, but by far and away the main centre for its manufacture was East Anglia. All this was about to change. Thanks to men like John Hustler of Bradford, Yorkshire would replace East Anglia as the country's principal manufacturer of worsted.

Hustler, born in 1714, became a master manufacturer and merchant, and later served on the Worsted Committee – a body set up by the manufacturers to regulate and police the industry in an attempt to combat mounting fraud and theft among suppliers and outworkers. The Worsted Acts of 1777 allowed for the establishment of an inspectorate whose job it was to investigate possible cases of fraud and, if necessary, bring the transgressors to court. Hustler had been involved with a combination of manufacturers between 1754 and 1776, and it was this experience that led to him being appointed chairman of the Yorkshire committee. The committee brought a measure of co-ordination to the industry that was to see trade continue to develop and put Yorkshire at the centre of the woollen and worsted industry.

By 1773 such was the importance of worsted to Bradford that local manufacturers clubbed together to pay for a Piece Hall specialising in the sale of this type of cloth. In 1779 Halifax opened its rather grand 315-room Piece Hall, but here dealers traded in both worsted and woollen cloths.

∞ THE FACTORY AGE ∞

The prospect of work in the new factories attracted thousands of people from rural areas to the textile towns of Lancashire and Yorkshire. Starting work in a factory in the early-nineteenth century would have been unlike anything they had known before. There were strict hours of attendance, working at a pace set by the employer in conditions that were virtually unregulated. People, including children, worked long hours – Bradford mill owners being among those who used orphans sent from London workhouses as little more than slave labour. Children as young as five worked up to 13 hours a day and were beaten to keep them awake.

Living conditions were often appalling. Families were crowded into single rooms or cellars and sanitation usually consisted of a cesspit, the contents of which invariably managed to contaminate the local water supply: a communal well. It took several outbreaks of cholera resulting in thousands of deaths to galvanise the country into public health measures.

Hand-weaving was considered a man's job. Power looms didn't make much of an impression in Bradford mills until the 1830s, but once the advantages were seen they soon took over, enabling women and girls to weave. Mechanization had long been viewed with suspicion by mill workers fearing for their jobs. This fear manifested itself in Luddism and the Luddites refused point blank to accept technical innovation.

The first serious problems occurred in 1811-12, when hand croppers rebelled against the introduction of shearing frames. Mills were attacked, frames destroyed and manufacturers threatened. Mill-owner William Horsfall was shot dead by Luddites on Crosland Moor. The Luddites were ruthlessly put down, with Horsfall's murderers paying with their lives on the gallows at York Castle.

In the 1820s violence erupted once more over the introduction of power looms and mechanical combing machines. In 1822 a power loom was smuggled into a mill at Shipley, but word soon got out and the place was surrounded by angry weavers. The loom was dismantled and taken away, but the cart on which it was being carried was attacked. The remains of the loom were dragged in triumph through the streets of Baildon.

There were attempts to improve working conditions in the the mill towns. Men such as Richard Oastler and John Wood petitioned parliament to cut factory hours and end child labour in the mills. By the 1850s some workers were getting a few days' holiday, even if it was without pay, and there was at least some time off at weekends.

A world away from industrial unrest was the Great Exhibition of 1851, which proved a hit with Bradford mill workers. Travel agent Thomas Cook would send his son from Derby to Bradford on a Friday with several trains of empty carriages. John then toured the streets in a van accompanied by a band and persuaded the workers to part with five shillings each for their train fares. It is said that the local pawnshops were full of watches, due to workers raising extra cash for spending money.

∞ TITUS SALT AND SAMUEL LISTER ∞

Between them Titus Salt and Samuel Lister were probably two of the most influential people in the history of Bradford. Titus Salt and his family moved to Bradford from Wakefield. Titus was apprenticed as a woolcomber, after which he landed a partnership with Daniel Salt & Son.

The story of how Titus made his fortune is well known, but it wasn't his first venture. Titus acquired a large shipment of Russian Donskoi wool, but found it impossible to sell on. Not to be outdone, he took over a mill and had the wool spun himself. The wool made an excellent yarn and sold without difficulty.

Titus' love affair with alpaca began when spotted some unwanted bales of the stuff in the warehouse. Taking a sample, he asked his father's opinion. His father advised him to leave well alone. Like most sons, Titus ignored his father's advice, bought the entire shipment and had it woven. Alpaca soon caught on and the Salts prospered.

What sets Titus apart from many other Bradford mill owners was his concern for the welfare of his workforce. Titus realised that a contented workforce meant better productivity and better productivity meant that he would continue to prosper. It all culminated in the building of a new mill and a village to house its workforce at Saltaire between 1850 and 1853. Titus provided his workers with a standard of accommodation far higher than most of them would ever have had in Bradford. He also built a school, almshouses and a cottage hospital, but no pubs as he was against alcohol.

Another well-known businessman was Samuel Cunliffe Lister who came from a mill and quarry-owning family. Samuel gave up the manufacturing side of the business for a while to concentrate on woolcombing and the development of machinery for the worsted trade.

He went into partnership with George Donnisthorpe, a mechanic from Leeds who had developed a woolcombing machine. Samuel knew that George's design could be improved on and in 1843 they produced their first samples of fine-combed Botany wool. They bought up most of the patents for combing machines and put theirs on the market. With profits of £1,000 per machine, Lister became a very wealthy man able to finance the building of his magnificent Manningham Mill. An enormous worsted and silk mill, Manningham had a total floor space of 26 acres. Its chimney, styled as an Italian campanile, is 255 ft high and is known as Lister's pride.

Between 1888 and 1893 the number of trades unionists almost doubled. In 1891 Bradford experienced a strike lasting five months, the reason being an imposed reduction in wages at Lister's mill due to a fall-off in orders. A meeting at St George's Hall ended with strikers clashing with police. The following night it is said that 20,000 people rioted and troops were called in to assist the civil powers. On the third night a searchlight was mounted on the tower of the town hall and troops were again called in. There were a number of baton charges and arrests made before the mob was finally dispersed. The strikers returned to work having gained nothing.

A direct result of the Lister's strike was the founding of the Independent Labour Party at a conference held in the town in 1893. Among those present was Keir Hardie, George Bernard Shaw and Fred Jowett.

∽ By Road, Rail and Canal ∽

The 127-mile long Leeds & Liverpool canal was one of the great civil-engineering projects of the eighteenth century. Authorised in 1770 the canal would, once completed, allow the passage of goods from the Mersey to the Humber. In 1778 three sections were open for traffic but due to problems with financing, construction came to a halt until a new money-raising Act was placed before Parliament in 1790.

Work slowed down again in 1792 following the outbreak of war with France, and the canal was not completed throughout until 1816. In spite of Bradford's growing importance, the nearest the canal got to the town was at Shipley. It was not until 1820 that a three-mile-long canal from Shipley to the centre of Bradford was opened.

There was a considerable amount of traffic between Bradford and Leeds, much of which was for onward shipment. Though the canal carried its fair share, the old Leeds-Bradford turnpike was extremely busy by the standards of the day and by 1830 was becoming increasingly difficult to maintain. In that year there was a proposal to link the two towns by rail with a line running through Laisterdyke, Stanningley and Wortley. The scheme was abandoned due to ever-increasing civil engineering estimates and hostility from landowners.

Bradford would not be served by a direct rail link until July 1846, when the Leeds & Bradford railway opened for traffic. Four years later the Lancashire & Yorkshire railway reached the town, followed in 1854 by the Great Northern railway. Bradford was never to be on a through route, though the Midland railway had planned to build a new line from Royston via the Spen Valley to link up with the Shipley-Bradford line. Some work was done but the project was finally killed off with the outbreak of the Great War.

DARLEY STREET, 1897.
Note the sign advertising the spectacle maker. These larger-than-life signs were used to great effect by Victorian shop keepers. Further on up the street is the public library, where a news room stayed open until 8pm.

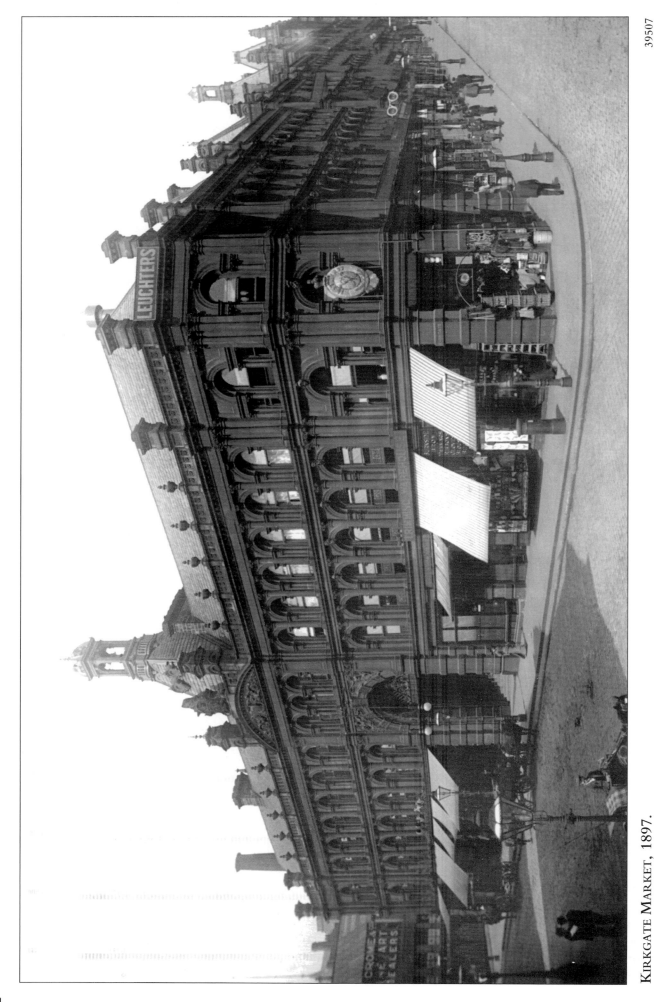

KIRKGATE MARKET, 1897.

In 1866 the council obtained the market rights from the Rawson family and built the Kirkgate Market, which was among the largest in the country. Nearby were the Rawson Market and an open market.

39507

POLICEMAN ON TRAFFIC DUTY, MARKET STREET, 1897. 39509
A hundred years earlier Bradford's 6,000 inhabitants were looked after by just two constables and a handful of deputies. There were also six night watchmen available, but they only patrolled property belonging to those willing to pay for the service.

WOOL EXCHANGE, 1897. 39513
On trading days the place could be truly international with buyers and sellers from around the world. It was said that no matter the type of wool or hair, a buyer would be found at the Bradford Exchange.

WOOL EXCHANGE, *c.*1897.

The Venetian Gothic-style Wool Exchange was completed in 1867. It is said when traders were about their buying and selling on Mondays and Thursdays, the place was akin to a madhouse.

TECHNICAL COLLEGE, 1890. 23495

In 1882 the college became independent from the Mechanics' Institute and was given its own premises. The college was seen as essential if Bradford was to keep abreast of competition from France in the production of quality wollen cloths.

INSTITUTE OF TECHNOLOGY, c.1965. B173072

In 1966 the institute was upgraded to a university. During the 1960s and 70s the college was expanded and a new regional college of art was built.

TYRRELL STREET, 1903.
On the left is Booth & Walker, one of Bradford's leading retail outlets famed for its china and glassware showrooms.

TOWN HALL, 1903.

The splendidly Gothic town hall on the right was completed in 1873 at a cost of £100,000. By the time this photo was taken, it is clearly showing the effects of thirty years' worth of industrial pollution. The building was given a thorough cleaning in the early 1970s.

49712

TOWN HALL, 1897.   39511

In April 1891, following two nights of trouble caused by strikers from Lister's factory, a searchlight was mounted on the tower of the town hall and troops were brought in to assist the civil powers. There were a number of baton charges and arrests made before the strikers were finally broken.

COUNCIL CHAMBER, 1888.   21009

An interior view of the gas-lit council chamber. It was designed by Lockwood and Mawson, who had already earned wide acclaim for Salt's Mill, Saltaire and the Wool Exchange.

TOWN HALL, 1888.

The Town Hall was built on land which was once in the township of Horton. In 1294 Henry de Lacy had obtained a charter to hold markets and fairs in Bradford. That same year de Lacy was in dispute with two other Norman lords over boundaries. De Lacy claimed land from Horton (the Turles; later Tyrrel Street), for his mill. Hugh de Horton was awarded an annual rent of 3s from de Lacy, his heirs and successors for the trouble.

VICTORIA SQUARE, 1950.
This shows the square just a few months before the abandonment of the tramway system in 1950. In the background a trolleybus is about to pass a tram as it heads towards the town hall.

B173028

VICTORIA SQUARE, *c.*1955.   B173030

In 1950 the woollen industry in Yorkshire employed around 150,000 people in 1,123 woollen and worsted mills. By 1967 there were 825 mills operating, but by 1986 the figure had dropped to just 172.

BRADFORD, *c.*1955.   B173031

As well as having to pay high wages, the Yorkshire woollen industry was facing tough competition from overseas manufacturers, who were starting to flood the market with yarn and fabrics due to the removal of import duties. The result was that many well-known firms went out of business.

FORSTER SQUARE, 1903.
In 1882 the Broadstones area was cleared to make way for Forster Square. Part of the redevelopment included a post office, which though impressive in its own right obscured the ascent to the parish church.

49711

CATHEDRAL, 1923.   74406

In December 1642, the Earl of Newcastle was approaching Bradford with a Royalist force. The town had declared for Parliament and the parish church was being fortified. The tower was protected from cannon shot with sheets of wool and it was here that the citizens made their stand.

OLD CHURCH NAVE EAST, 1890.   23499

During the Civil War, Francis Corker, Vicar of Bradford and a devout Royalist helped to save Pontefract Castle from being taken by Parliament. He later worked as a spy but was captured and imprisoned at Lincoln. Escaping on the eve of his execution, he eventually died in 1667.

PARISH CHURCH, 1891.
The town's population by 1891 was around 216,000. The increase had been so rapid that there was a serious shortage of housing. The council had no alternative but to allow a temporary relaxation of building regulations so that a large number of back-to-back houses could be put up quickly.

28297

FORSTER SQUARE, 1897.
On the right is the statue of Richard Oastler, who was the leading advocate for the end to child labour in the mills. Children often worked 13 hours a day in Bradford's factories and were subjected to beatings to keep them awake. Just sneaking into views to the right of the statue is a steam tram engine. These noisy smoke-belching machines were an interim measure between horse-trams and a viable electric street tramway system.

POST OFFICE, *c.*1955.

Cathedral status had been granted to the parish church in 1920 but work on upgrading and extending the building did not begin until the 1950s. Among the improvements were a new chancel, song room, and a vestry for the bishop.

FORSTER SQUARE, *c.*1955.

Named after William Edward Forster (1818-1886), MP for Bradford and the minister responsible for the 1870 Education Act, which established compulsory state elementary education.

FORSTER SQUARE, *c.*1965. B173068
The changing face of Bradford. Victorian grandeur gives way to twentieth century functionalism. Enough said.

VICTORIA HOTEL, 1897. 39521
The Great Northern Railway opened its terminus at Adolphus Street in 1854, but from 1867 shared a joint station (Bradford Exchange) with the Lancashire & Yorkshire. Rooms at the Victoria Hotel cost from 4s a night.

St George's Hall, 1897.
39517
In 1891 the hall was the scene of a crowded meeting of strikers from Lister's. A slump had led to a massive reduction in wages and many were suffering. Following the meeting strikers clashed with police. Until the Town Hall was finished St George's Hall was used for any council business where large numbers of people were expected to turn up.

CHILDREN'S HOSPITAL, 1897.   39523

Throughout much of the nineteenth century, Bradford's death rate among children under five years of age was a disgrace. In 1876 alone over 2,000 of Bradford's under-fives died.

THE INFIRMARY, 1897.   39522

During rounds the patients had to lay in their beds at attention and were not supposed to speak to the doctor or matron unless asked a specific question.

THE ALHAMBRA, *c.*1955.
The trolleybus was developed on the Continent. Like the electric tramcar, it drew current from an overhead power supply but did not require rails to run on. On 20 June 1911, a joint scheme between Leeds and Bradford saw the inauguration of the first trolleybus service in Great Britain.

B173043

THE ALHAMBRA AND NEW VICTORIA, *c.*1955.   B173009

It was on a site near where the Alhambra stands that Bradford's first spinning mill was completed in 1800. In 1804 it was almost destroyed by fire.

WAR MEMORIAL, 1923.   74404

Behind the memorial is the statue of Queen Victoria, unveiled by HRH The Prince of Wales in 1904 during his visit to the Bradford Exhibition.

MANNINGHAM LANE, 1921. 71623

Seventy years earlier, Thomas Cook's son had wandered the streets of Bradford, enticing workers to part with the five-shilling train fare for a trip to London to see the Great Exhibition. It is said that the local pawnshops were full of watches left by workers raising the fare and perhaps a little spending money.

MANNINGHAM LANE, 1902.
The building on the left where the men with the ladders are working is the Theatre Royal. It was here on 13th October 1905 that Sir Henry Irving gave his last performance. After retiring to his hotel for the night he was taken ill and died.

48570

MANNINGHAM LANE, *c.*1950.
The trams have been replaced by trolleybuses and though Bradford was a pioneer of trolleybus operation, the first-ever conversion of an existing route from trams to trolleys was in Birmingham in 1922.

B173020

LISTER PARK, 1921.   71624
This photo shows the entrance to Lister (Manningham) Park.

LISTER PARK GATEWAY, 1897.   39524
In 1870 Samuel Lister offered his Manningham Park estate to the Corporation for £40,000, a fraction of what it was really worth.

CARTWRIGHT MEMORIAL HALL, c.1955.
The Cartwright Memorial Hall was opened in 1904 on the site formerly occupied by Samuel Lister's mansion. Named in honour of Edmund Cartwright (1743-1823), the hall houses the City Art Gallery and Museum.

BOATING ON THE LAKE, LISTER PARK, 1921.
"Come in no 23, your time's up!"

71629

THE LAKE, LISTER PARK, *c.*1955.

B173021

In May 1904, Bradford turned out to welcome the Prince and Princess of Wales when they came to Lister Park to open the Bradford Exhibition. The lake was the venue for naval battles using scaled-down models of warships (a similar event still takes place on the lake at Scarborough during the summer season).

LISTER PARK, 1897.

39527

The 1904 Exhibition attracted 2.5 million visitors. Temporary buildings erected in the park included a concert hall and a pavilion. There was also a Somali village complete with inhabitants.

LISTER PARK BANDSTAND, 1923.
The crowds gather in this picture for an afternoon concert.

74400

PEEL PARK, 1897.   39529

Bradford's first public park was Peel Park, opened in 1863 and named in honour of Sir Robert Peel, who had been instrumental in the abolition of the Corn Laws.

PEEL PARK, 1897.   39530

In 1874 the park was the venue for celebrations, including a spectacular fireworks display, to mark the unveiling of a statue to Sir Titus Salt. When the park was first mooted, Sir Titus gave £1,000 towards the cost.

CHAPTER 2

∾ AROUND BRADFORD ∾

∾ QUEENSBURY ∾

Lying to the south-west of Bradford at 1,100 ft above sea level is Queensbury. The town was originally called Queen's Head but the name was changed during the nineteenth century. Queensbury is the home of Foster's Black Dyke Mill, which opened in 1835

∾ SALTAIRE ∾

Saltaire owes its existence to Sir Titus Salt, who moved his alpaca and mohair mills here in the 1850s. Sir Titus was determined that his workers should have a healthier environment to live and work in. The workers' cottages he had built were made of stone, lined with brick, and comprised a parlour, kitchen, pantry and from two to four bedrooms. When the village was completed there were 850 houses and 45 almshouses, as well as civic buildings. Being a strict temperance man, Titus refused to allow the construction of public houses in Saltaire and the town remains 'dry' to this day. Though Titus was concerned for the welfare of his employees, he expected them to put in a fair day's work for their pay.

∾ BAILDON ∾

Situated one-and-a-half-miles north of Shipley, Baildon straddles a hilltop on the edge of Baildon Moor. It was through the streets of this old industrial town in 1822 that rioters dragged the remains of a power loom after the cart on which it was being carried was attacked.

∾ SHIPLEY ∾

A centre for weaving and the scene of a near riot in 1822 when James Warbrick erected a power loom in a mill. The loom had been smuggled in but word soon got out and the mill was surrounded by a mob of weavers. The loom was dismantled but the cart carrying it away was attacked and the loom destroyed. It was at Shipley that the three-mile-long Bradford canal joined the Leeds & Liverpool canal.

BLACK DYKE MILLS, QUEENSBURY, *c*.1960.   Q15007

The entrance to John Foster's Black Dyke Mill. Like Titus Salt, Foster saw benefits to be had from promoting alpaca and both enjoyed a virtual monopoly with this type of cloth until others followed their lead.

THE MEMORIAL, QUEENSBURY, *c*.1960.   Q15010

The Black Dyke Mill brass band owes its origins to none other than John Foster. Foster was a keen horn player in the local brass band and when it looked as if it might fold, he made it the work's official band.

HIGH STREET, QUEENSBURY, c.1960.
The reason the picture is devoid of people is that it was probably going to be used as a postcard. If you look to the left of the lamp standard you can see that a car has been brushed-out. Frith's reasoning behind this was that fashions tended to date postcards very quickly; this way they would be able to keep it on sale for a longer period.

HOLY TRINITY CHURCH, QUEENSBURY, *c.*1960.

Among the interesting churches in the Bradford area is St James' Church, Tong. Built in 1727, a Norman arch and a fifteen century window survive from an older church. Inside little has changed over the last 270 years or so. There are box pews, fine panelling and a three-decker pulpit. Another church of interest is All Souls, Haley Hill, Boothtown which was rebuilt in 1856-59 and is probably one of Sir Gilbert Scott's finest pieces of work.

Q15016

OLD RAGGALDS INN, QUEENSBURY, *c.*1960.

This inn offered Webster's fine ales. In the late 1990s the only Queensbury pub to make it into the *Good Beer Guide* is the *New Dolphin*, Ambler Thorp Road. There are quite a number from Bradford, including; *The Blue Pig, The Castle, The Corn Dolly, The Fighting Cock, The Goldsborough, Haigy's, the Melborn Hotel, The New Beehive* and *The Oakleigh.*

Q15013

54

SALTAIRE STATION, 1909.   61871
Saltaire station is on the Midland line from Bradford to Skipton. Salts Mill, some six-storeys high, was built next to the line. The official opening of the mill took place in 1853 when 3,500 people attended a banquet held in the combing shed.

SALTS MILL, SALTAIRE, 1903. 49705

When opened it was the largest mill in Europe: the weaving shed housed 1,200 looms and the workforce was in excess of 3,000. In 1903 around 259,000 people were employed in the UK wool industry.

SALTAIRE, 1893. 33186

Salt's rules for workers living here were strict. Washing was not allowed to be hung out to dry (wash-houses were provided with wringing machines and drying closets). Also there were no public houses.

VICTORIA ROAD, SALTAIRE, 1893.
As well as building Saltaire, Titus Salt donated well over £100,000 to various causes around Bradford.

VICTORIA ROAD, SALTAIRE, 1909.
Saltaire's streets were named after members of Titus Salt's family.

THE INSTITUTE, SALTAIRE, 1893.

The institute contained a library, reading rooms, gymnasium and a billiards room. There were two lions outside and two more across the road outside the school. The lions were to have graced Nelson's Column but were considered to be too small.

33192

SALT SCHOOL, SALTAIRE, 1903.
49704

One of the school's famous pupils was Joseph Wright, who from the age of seven worked at Salts mill. When he got older, Joseph enrolled at the Bradford Mechanics' Institute and later at the Yorkshire College. He was admitted to Heidelberg University, where he gained a doctorate and he went on to become Professor of Comparative Philology at Oxford.

THE RIVER AIRE, SALTAIRE, 1893.
33191

By the 1860s the river was already suffering from the effects of pollution due to it being used as an open sewer by Bradford's mills. In 1868 the corporation was successfully sued for failing to take steps to control waste disposal. The outcome of the case was the opening of Esholt Sewage Works.

SALTAIRE PARK, 1909.
Apart from the ladies with the perambulator, the park appears to be deserted in this picture. It might have been a requirement that the Frith cameraman take the picture with as few people as possible in it. This was often done at this time purely for commercial rather than artistic reasons.

61872

71288

DICK HUDSON'S PUB, BAILDON, 1921.

On the edge of the moors stands Hudson's pub, or to give it its old name, The Fleece Inn. In the nineteenth century, landlord Dick Hudson was renowned for his ham and eggs. People visiting the moors would call after an invigorating walk and eat their fill.

VIEW FROM THE BANK, BAILDON, c.1960.
The town is situated on a hilltop one and a half miles north of Shipley. An electric tramway was built to assist access to the higher reaches of Baildon Moor. The summer service was frequent owing to the popularity of the area. A restricted winter service operated mainly for the benefit of local residents.

B33020

St Paul's Church, Shipley, 1893.
When Titus Salt died in 1876 thousands lined the route of his funeral cortege from Bradford Town Hall to Shipley. A staunch tea-totaller and Congregationalist, Sir Titus was not buried at Shipley, but in a mausoleum at the Congregational Church, Saltaire, opposite his mill.

33195

SHIPLEY PARK, 1903.
Here you can see the tower of St Paul's in the background. It was at the church in 1928 that the funeral of Handel Parker took place. Handel worked as a woolcomber but left when he was 20 to become a full-time musician. One of his most famous tunes is *Deep Harmony*, which the Black Dyke Mill's band always played at the end of every concert.

49701

ARNDALE SHOPPING CENTRE, SHIPLEY, *c.*1965.

The shopping centre contrasts strongly with the older retail outlets and civic buildings of the town.

KIRKGATE, SHIPLEY, *c.*1965.

Most of the town's older properties are built from dark stone.

SHIPLEY, 1909.
As there were no pubs in Saltaire, those residents in need of sustenance could find it in Shipley, though they could expect no mercy if brought up on charges of drunkenness before Titus Salt, who was also one of Bradford's leading magistrates.

61865

THE ROUNDABOUT, SHIPLEY, c.1965.   S122012

In the background are the former tram sheds, converted to house Shipley's complement of trolleybuses. Bradford was not only the first place in the country, it was also the last. The system survived until 1972 when it was finally closed.

MANOR HOUSE, SHIPLEY, 1903.   49699

In the eleventh century there was over 150 manors in the area between the Aire and Calder, Pontefract and Clitheroe. They all passed into the hands of Ilbert de Lacy, William the Conqueror's man in those parts in recognition for his part in suppressing a revolt in 1070.

THE GLEN, SHIPLEY, 1909.   61867
Despite this view, Bradford was always short of water and it was the lack of the stuff that inspired mill owners to switch to steampower. Many mills sank their own wells to ensure continuous supplies.

THE GLEN, SHIPLEY, 1921.
Shipley Glen did for Bradford what Roundhay Park did for Leeds. It was the nearest open country to Bradford where people could escape from the smoke and the grime. At weekends Bradford Corporation Tramways laid on extra services to cope with the number of people making for Shipley Glen.

THE GLEN, SHIPLEY, 1909.
Water is vital in wool processing and the softer it is the better the finished product.

HARROGATE ROAD, GREENGATES, *c*.1955.   G115010

On the right is the local branch of the Co-op, a movement said to have begun in Rochdale with just 28 members and capital of just £28. What would have been the retailer's profit after all expenses was handed back to the membership as a dividend.

NEW LINE, GREENGATES, *c*.1955.   G115009

Straight ahead at the crossroads is New Line, while to the left of Glovers is Harrogate Road.

THE CANAL, GREENGATES, c.1960.
At 127 miles in length, the Leeds & Liverpool canal took over 40 years to complete and cost in excess of £1million. The canal was authorised in 1770 and within 8 years three sections were open for traffic.

APPERLEY LOCKS, GREENGATES, *c.*1955.
From Shipley the canal makes a long swing round a 500 ft-high hill to Apperley Bridge. Halfway round the curve a set of three locks lowers the canal by 25 ft. Just beyond the Mitchell swing bridge the Dobson Locks lower it a further 23 ft.

G115013

Pictorial Memories Collection

A great new range of publications featuring the work of innovative Victorian photographer Francis Frith.

∞ 1998 Titles ∞

County Series   £9.99

1-84125-045-7	Berkshire	
053-8	Buckinghamshire	
024-4	Derbyshire	
077-5	Greater London	
028-7	Kent	
029-5	Lake District	
051-1	Lancashire	
031-7	Leicestershire	
026-0	London	
027-9	Norfolk	
030-9	Sussex	
063-5	West Yorkshire	
025-2	Yorkshire	

Town & City Series   £9.99

010-4	Brighton & Hove	
015-5	Canterbury	
079-1	Edinburgh	
012-0	Glasgow & Clydeside	
081-3	Norwich	
040-6	York	

Country Series   £9.99

1-84125-075-9	Ireland	
071-6	North Wales	
073-2	Scotland	
069-4	South Wales	

Poster Books   £4.99

000-7	Canals and Waterways	
032-5	Derbyshire	
001-5	High Days and Holidays	
036-8	Kent	
037-6	Lake District	
034-1	London	
005-8	Railways	

£5.99

023-6	Canterbury	
043-0	Derby	

∞ Titles from January to July 1999 ∞

County Series   £9.99

1-84125-049-x	Warwickshire	March	
047-3	Staffordshire		
057-0	Devon		
067-8	Cheshire		
065-1	Nottinghamshire		
059-7	Cornwall		

1-84125-101-1	Surrey		
095-3	Hampshire		
128-3	Highlands	April	
149-6	Hertfordshire		
130-5	North Yorkshire	May	
150-x	Wiltshire		

Town & City Series   £7.99

089-9	Maidstone	March	
087-2	Bradford		
083-x	Colchester		
093-7	Dublin		
091-0	Leeds		
105-4	Buxton		
111-9	Bristol		
113-5	Nottingham		
011-2	Manchester		
107-0	Matlock		
009-0	Macclesfield	April	
132-1	St Ives		
008-2	Derby		
113-x	Sevenoaks		
014-7	Newbury		
134-8	Bognor Regis		
144-5	Leicester		
145-3	East Grinstead		
146-1	Newark		

137-2	Sheffield	May	
138-0	Cambridge		
139-9	Penzance		
140-2	Eastbourne		
147-x	Llandudno		
142-9	Torquay		
148-8	Whitby		
159-3	Scarborough	June	
160-7	Faversham to Herne Bay		
164-x	Scilly Isles		
162-3	Dorset Coast		
168-2	Falmouth		
165-8	Newquay		
154-2	Bakewell	July	
163-1	Lincoln		
167-4	Barnstaple		
174-7	Great Yarmouth		
141-0	Blackpool		
207-7	Dartmoor		

WATERTON PRESS, WATERTON ESTATE, BRIDGEND, GLAMORGAN, CF31 3XP.
TEL: 01656 668836   FAX: 01656 668710

Voucher

This voucher entitles you to a half price mounted print
normally £19.95

*Mounted prints are A4 sepia, mounted in a cream mount with beval cut aperture and single burgundy ruled line, greyboard backing and cello bagged.

Special offer price £9.97

Simply select the view in this book that you would like to receive as a mounted print, and complete the form below.

Page & Negative Number	Town & Description

I enclose a cheque/postal order for £9.97 which includes p&p, made payable to "The Francis Frith Collection."

Name & Address:

Mr/Mrs/Miss/Ms

Initial   Surname

Address

Town

County

Postcode

Daytime Telephone No.
(incase of queries)

Send your voucher and remittance to:
The Francis Frith Collection
Dept FF026, 'Friths Barn', Teffont,
Salisbury, Wilts, SP3 5QP.